A BASIC BOOK OF BUDGERIGARS LOOK-AND-LEARN

by
T. HALABURDA

Photographs and Illustrations: David Alderton, Louise Bauck, H. Bielfeld, Michael DeFreitas, Michael Gilroy, Jon Gleason, Ray Hanson, Keith Hindwood, B. Kahl, Harry V. Lacey, A.F. Lydon, Susan C. Miller, Ron & Val Moat, Robert Pearcy, J.R. Quinn, L. Robinson, Vince Serbin, M. Shipman, Louise Van der Meid, Norma Veitch, Wayne Wallace

Distributed in the UNITED STATES to the Pet Trade by T.F.H. Publications, Inc., One T.F.H. Plaza, Neptune City, NJ 07753; distributed in the UNITED STATES to the Bookstore and Library Trade by National Book Network, Inc. 4720 Boston Way, Lanham MD 20706; in CANADA to the Pet Trade by H & L Pet Supplies Inc., 27 Kingston Crescent, Kitchener, Ontario N2B 2T6; Rolf C. Hagen Ltd., 3225 Sartelon Street, Montreal 382 Quebec; in CANADA to the Book Trade by Macmillan of Canada (A Division of Canada Publishing Corporation), 164 Commander Boulevard, Agincourt, Ontario M1S 3C7; in the United Kingdom by T.F.H. Publications, PO Box 15, Waterlooville PO7 6BQ; in AUSTRALIA AND THE SOUTH PACIFIC by T.F.H. (Australia), Pty. Ltd., Box 149, Brookvale 2100 N.S.W., Australia; in NEW ZEALAND by Brooklands Aquarium Ltd. 5 McGiven Drive, New Plymouth, RD1 New Zealand; in Japan by T.F.H. Publications, Japan—Jiro Tsuda, 10-12-3 Ohjidai, Sakura, Chiba 285, Japan; in SOUTH AFRICA by Multipet Pty. Ltd., P.O. Box 35347, Northway, 4065, South Africa. Published by T.F.H. Publications, Inc.
Manufactured in the United States of America by T.F.H. Publications, Inc.

SUGGESTED READING

T.F.H. offers the most comprehensive selections of books dealing with pet birds. A selection of significant titles is presented here; they and the thousands of other animal books published by T.F.H. are available at the same place you bought this one, or write to us for a free catalog.

T.F.H. Publications
One T.F.H. Plaza
Third & Union Avenues
Neptune, NJ 07753

SUGGESTED READING

INTRODUCTION

The budgerigar is the most popular pet bird today. It has the most established mutations of any species, resulting in its many different color forms. Also, the affordability and the ease of breeding budgies make it widely available. Not only is it beautiful, it is also very intelligent, easy to tame and a good talker. The budgerigar is hardy and active and is highly recommended as a first bird.

This bird shows the true coloration of the budgerigar. Notice the black spots on the throat and the blue tipped cheek feathers.

These are just two examples of the color variations available. These beautiful mutations are just one reason for budgies' overwhelming popularity.

Today many people still refer to them as parakeets; however, the term parakeet could refer to a number of small parrot species.

Budgerigars are about 7 inches in length and live for an average of ten years. Their true or wild coloration is mostly green, with a yellow head area. The nape and back are yellow, barred with black, and the tail is blue. There are a series of dark spots on the throat, and the cheek feathers are tipped with a violet-blue.

◆ The scientific name for the budgerigar is, *Melopsittacus undulatus. Melopsittacus* being derived from the Greek language meaning 'song parrot' and *undulatus* being Latin for 'wavy-lined', which refers to the dark barred pattern of the back and wings.

HISTORY

Budgerigars, *Melopsittacus undulatus*, are distributed throughout Australia, but not onto Tasmania. They form huge flocks and spend a great deal of time on the ground searching for seeds. They are colony breeders, usually breeding between the months of August and December. However, they will breed just about any time during the year following the rains. They utilize hollows in trees, fallen logs and fence posts as nesting sites. Some decayed wood, barely lining the bottom of a concave area in the nest site, is as far as their nest building activities go. These birds were first discovered in 1840 by the British ornithologist John Gould. He transported live specimens back to England where they quickly became popular.

◆ This illustration shows the wild coloration of the budgerigar.

HISTORY

Budgerigars are found mainly in the interior regions of Australia where they inhabit open forests and wooded areas near water.

Once budgies' diet and nesting habits were correctly identified by ornithologists and bird keepers, they bred successfully in captivity.

The budgerigar is a nomadic bird, following water and grass seed availability.

They became readily available and reasonably affordable, making them popular throughout Europe and the United States.

A wild budgerigar in its native homeland.

The word *budgerigar* comes from the Aboriginal word *'Betcherrygah'* meaning 'good to eat'.

SELECTION

Whether you are looking for a bird as a pet, for breeding stock or for exhibition, choosing a healthy specimen is the most important aspect of your selection. Most pet shops will have assorted stock available continually. If looking for a pet, it is best to purchase a young bird of about 5 or 6 weeks old. It will be easier for you to form a bond with, tame and teach to talk. The most notable sign in selecting a young bird is the striped pattern starting at the cere (the fleshy area around the nostrils) and continuing back along the head.

Choosing a healthy bird is more important than choosing one just for its coloration.

These two are perfect examples of healthy birds. Notice the clear eyes and smooth, clean feathers.

Also, the tail will be shorter in younger birds. Before making a selection, check the establishment for cleanliness and the general health of all the birds. If the cages, perches and dishes are dirty and soiled, you should avoid making a purchase and look elsewhere. Cleanliness is important to a bird's health.

If the surroundings are satisfactory, first observe the birds from a distance so that you may watch their activity. Avoid birds that are inactive or unhealthy looking.

This illustration shows the ideal conformation and quality of the budgerigar. You will need help and practice at first to determine what makes a quality exhibition specimen.

This bird shows a full breast area. Before purchasing, check the breast area to make sure the breast bone is not protruding; an underweight bird can have a serious illness.

There are so many color varieties to choose from that you may have difficulty choosing just one.

The beak should be smooth as pictured here, with the upper mandible lying smoothly over the lower. Do not select a bird if the mandibles are crossed or extremely overgrown.

SELECTION

Next, take a closer look. Choose a bird that is alert and active, not one that seems uninterested in the activities around it. Check the eyes to make sure that they are bright and clear, with no discharge present. The cere and nostrils should be smooth and free of discharge and not puffy or swollen. The feet should grip the perch firmly; look to see that all toes are present. There are four toes, two facing forward and two backward. The feathers should be clean and smooth, with no bare patches. Make sure the vent area is clean, with no droppings stuck to the feathers.

Your pet dealer can either provide birds for you or direct you to another source. Select healthy stock, preferably proven pairs, meaning that they have a successful breeding history and have reared quality chicks. Birds from 1 to 4 years are best. The seller can tell you the age; they should be banded with dated information of when they were born. The seller should also be able to tell you about the offspring produced. The more information you receive the better.

Budgies are not expensive so you should always be able to purchase quality birds.

If looking to show your birds, seek the advice of exhibitors and breeders, for many are involved in both aspects of the hobby. This is a Pied Yellow Light Green Budgerigar.

Young birds such as these are recognizable by their dark beak coloring and the striped pattern starting above the cere. This is the best age to purchase a bird if looking for a tame companion.

How many birds you purchase for breeding stock will depend on your interest, space, time and money.

Always purchase the best birds you can afford. It is advised to start with a few pairs or maybe even a few cocks with twice as many hens. Since they are very social, they need the stimulus of others to start in their breeding activities. For exhibition birds, gather as much information as possible from bird shows, clubs and breeders. Good breeding birds may not necessarily make good show birds and the opposite holds true as well. Expect to pay more for quality exhibition stock. Once you have purchased a healthy specimen, you are on your way to enjoying the friendly and fascinating budgerigar.

When selecting breeding stock, stick to one or two color varieties; this will increase your chances of successful color breeding.

VARIETIES

A mutation is a change in a hereditary characteristic. Genes are the carriers of this information which is passed on from one generation to another. This information is generally predictable but from time to time it will change. How or why a gene mutates is not fully understood and it is not a common occurrence. In the wild not many mutations are seen, if the mutation does not benefit the species it will die out.

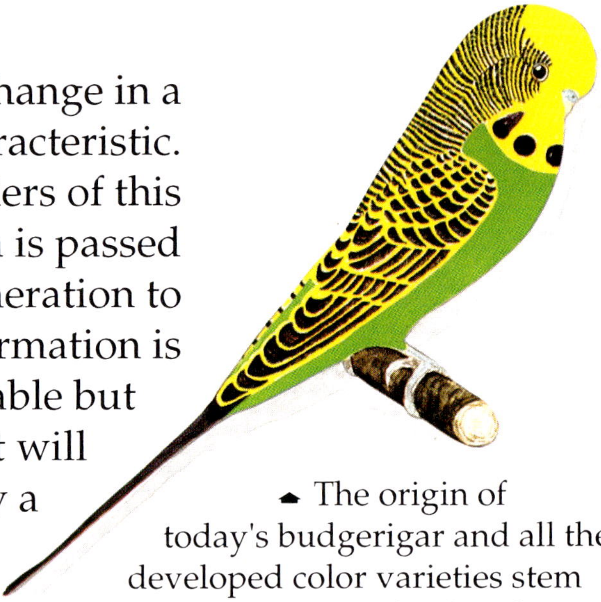

The origin of today's budgerigar and all the developed color varieties stem from the normal colored budgie as pictured here.

This is a gray Feather Duster mutation. The feathers create an inability to function normally; many Feather Dusters are unable to see because their feathers impair their vision. These birds are very short lived.

Notice the multi-colored markings on this Mosaic Budgerigar.

VARIETIES

Color mutations in the wild usually mark the bird out, making it more conspicuous; therefore it is easily spotted and subject to fall prey. In captivity these dangers are absent, so through selective breeding, when a mutation suddenly appears, it can be maintained if desired.

A variety of the green series is the Lutino mutation, which has no color pigments present. These birds have red eyes, yellow-orange beaks and the cere in the male is pale pink or violet.

This Yellow-winged Light Green variety does not have all yellow wings, but the primary flights are gray, as are the throat spots. The tail feathers are a light blue-gray.

This yellow cock is distinguished from the Lutino variety by having dark eyes rather than red ones.

VARIETIES

This is an example of the Opaline Violet variety. In opaline birds the lack of melanin is most noticeable on the head and neck area.

There are many color combinations and it can be confusing to understand how they are established and maintained. A more detailed study is necessary to achieve full understanding for breeding purposes. There are two categories in which color mutations are grouped. The first is the Green series, which is like that of the wild form. The second is the Blue series in which colors and patterns are developed through the mutation loss of the yellow color pigment. There is one oddity that occurs, belonging to neither series. It is called the Half-sider, which shows green on one side and blue on the other. It can not be maintained for it is not a true mutation but more of a phenomenon. There are also other mutations which affect the feathers, such as budgerigars with crests and specimens having long feathers as seen in the Feather Duster variety.

These birds are called Opaline Cinnamon-Gray-Green. Notice the cinnamon colored markings on the wings and tail.

VARIETIES

This is a dominant Pied Gray Budgerigar. Dominant pieds were originally from Holland and were the first pied forms of budgerigars. ➧

⬆ These pied budgerigar varieties are some of the most beautiful colored specimens available.

A budgerigar of the Pied Blue variety. ⬇

⬆ The bird on the left is a Cobalt and the one on the right is a Cobalt Pied variety. The pied factor indicates an absence of color in certain areas.

VARIETIES

Budgerigars with cinnamon coloring are one of the most popular show birds. Cinnamons will always have brownish primary feathers with the tail feathers being a violet blue. This is a Cinnamon Light Blue variety. Yellow pigmentation is not present in birds belonging to the blue series. This is the reason for the color changes in these varieties. ➧

➧ One of the most fulfilling aspects of the budgerigar hobby, to many breeders, is color breeding. The Cobalt White-wing is a variety of the blue series. In blue budgies, the yellow areas are replaced by white.

In the blue series, there are many different shades and combinations. The Light Blue Gray-wing has gray markings on the throat, head, back and wings, while the tail is a grayish blue. The cheek patches are a light violet. ➧

VARIETIES

The Pied Dark Green Budgerigar shows mostly yellow with the underbelly and rump a dark green. Most pied hens will have dark patches on their backs and wings.

Cinnamon Budgerigars are known for having dense plumage and are often used in improving those of other varieties.

Gray-green varieties are big winners at exhibitions, for they tend to be large birds with a broad head, which is considered a favorable characteristic.

DETERMINING AGE

There are certain characteristics that will enable you to distinguish a young bird from a mature bird. This can be especially helpful if looking for a companion bird. It is best to purchase a young one of about 5 or 6 weeks old. At this age it will be more receptive to you and easier to tame.

This mature female is distinguished by the dark brown colored cere and the absence of striping on the forehead.

The most easily recognizable trait is the striped pattern in the feathers just above the cere. Young birds will have this pattern running across the head from the cere to the nape. After about ten weeks of age these stripes will begin to fade and as adults, they will have the stripes only from the eye to the nape. The cere color will differ from that of mature birds. In young hens, the cere is a bluish-white color with the inside nostrils having a white border. In the adult, the cere is a chalky white color or a dark brown. On male birds, the youngsters have a pinkish cere with the adult having a prominent blue one.

The bright blue cere and light colored iris will let you know that this is an adult male.

These youngsters exhibit the dark pupil and iris as well as dark stripes from the neck up to the cere. There are however, certain color varieties where the barred pattern on the forehead is absent.

DETERMINING AGE

After the first moult, it will be almost impossible to tell the birds age.

As a youngster, this bird's throat spots were hardly visible. Their shape was crescent rather than full and round as they are now.

Youngsters may also have black markings on the upper beak. The eye is also an area to observe to help you determine age. In young birds both the iris and pupil are black. After about twelve weeks of age the iris will begin to lighten to a gray with the pupil remaining black.

The exception to these determining characteristics are birds that are Harlequin Pied, in which case the iris will remain black and the cere in the male will stay pink instead of turning blue.

The young begin the moulting process at about 12 to 16 weeks of age. The moulting process will last about 4 to 5 months and after which it will wear adult plumage.

Lutino varieties lack dark pigmentation so they will show no dark throat spots as a juvenile or an adult. Also in the Lutino, as well as Albino and Harlequin Pied, the cere color will remain light in the males rather than turning blue.

CAGES

There are a number of cages available in different sizes, styles and colors. Cages of wire with a removable bottom tray for easy cleaning are recommended. Plastic trays are easier to clean and maintain than metal ones. Purchase the largest cage suitable for a budgie that you can afford. Be careful, there are many cages that are too small, and these active little birds need room to stretch their wings and flutter about. Exercise is very important to the well being of your bird.

If possible, the cage should be longer than it is high. Stay away from the pagoda style of cage. Even though it is tall and looks roomy, the bird can only climb up and down and there is no room for any flight.

◆ Cage bars should not only be situated vertically, but horizontally as well. This will allow the bird to climb about the cage.

◆ It is important to supply your bird with a few perches as well as a couple of items to keep it occupied. Make sure you do not over clutter; allow the bird ample room to move about. This is a nice uncluttered cage.

CAGES

Before bringing your new bird home, you should have its cage set up with all the necessities ready and waiting.

The bars of the cage should be spaced so that it is impossible for the bird to stick its head through. If you plan on keeping more than one or two birds in the home, you may want to consider an indoor flight cage, which is larger and gives the birds more room.

Whatever style you choose, make sure that it is the most beneficial and roomiest for your bird. There are cages available that are beautiful to look at but will not be best suited for your pet's needs.

Either a bird gym or cage equipped with a playpen top will be beneficial. This provides the bird with an unconfined play area.

There are many types of indoor cages and flight areas for the single or multi budgerigar owner.

ACCESSORIES AND TOYS

To keep the budgie healthy and happy and to prevent boredom, there are many accessories available to furnish the cage. When doing so, be careful not to overcrowd it, leaving room for the bird to move about. Most cages will come with the bare necessities such as feed and water dishes as well as perches. Make sure the perches are wood, either dowels or natural branches, NO PLASTIC. You should also make sure that the perches are of varying sizes for the sake of the bird's feet. Other additions are beneficial to its well being such as cuttlebones, mineral blocks, bird baths, as well as recreational items like swings, ladders and colorful toys. Through trial and error you will find out what your bird enjoys most.

Branches of willow and fruit trees make great perches; the varying widths will keep the foot muscles exercised. The branches will also give the birds an opportunity to gnaw, helping to keep the beak trimmed as well as the claws.

A cuttlebone will help keep the bird's beak trim as well as providing extra calcium.

A wooden swing and ladder will provide your bird with lots of fun and exercise.

Giving a bird the opportunity to bathe by providing a bird bath is important in keeping the plumage looking clean and shiny.

ACCESSORIES AND TOYS

Some birds are totally amazed by mirrors and will spend large amounts of time staring and talking to their reflections.

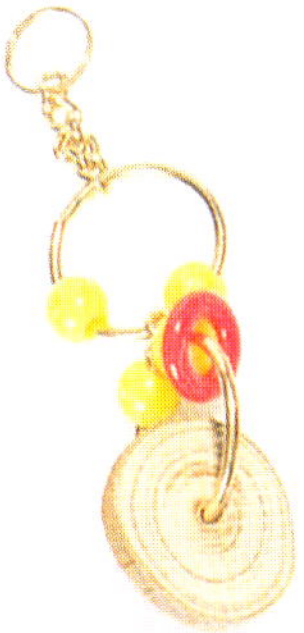

Popular items such as these will help keep a bird from becoming bored and lonely.

A treat holder for green food is just one of many items available through local pet stores.

This plastic ball with a bell inside will keep this budgie occupied for a long time. If the bird starts splintering the plastic, it's time for a new, heavier toy.

This bird is having fun with its penguin pal. Toys like this should not be offered to the bird on its cage bottom, for it will become soiled with droppings. This toy is better for play times when the bird is outside its cage.

AVIARIES

There are many different styles and sizes of aviaries. The one you choose will largely depend on your goals as an aviculturist, as well as space availability and affordability. Build the best aviary you can afford. It does not pay to skimp in this area; you will want one to last a long time.

The aviary consists of an enclosed area, to protect the birds from the elements, and a flight area. Be sure to build the structure on even, dry ground. A floor of dirt is the least desirable because it is hard to keep clean and free from bacteria. Stone or cement is preferred.

It is a good idea to visit different aviaries to look at different designs to see which one might best fit your needs.

Situate the aviary so that it is visible from the house and if possible, facing the south to protect against northerly winds.

Budgerigars are social birds and make an excellent aviary choice.

AVIARIES

The aviary should be constructed so that rodents and other mammals cannot burrow or squeeze their way in to bother your birds. ➧

Cover part of the flight with a clear waterproof covering to protect against the elements. The enclosed area should be equipped with heat, depending on where you live, and a light that has a dimmer. Birds will become frightened at the sudden turning off or on of the lights. They may become panicked and injure themselves by flying into something, or you may possibly strand a bird outside in the flight area. Perches of wood, preferably natural branches, need to be placed throughout the flight area. Feed dishes may be best placed in the enclosed sheltered area in case of bad weather, but do not situate them directly underneath perches so that they become soiled. An aviary can be more than just a place to house your birds; it can be an added attraction to any landscape with a little thought and planning.

▲ Do not build the aviary under any trees. This will only allow wild birds and other mammals to perch above and possibly taunt and upset the occupants.

▼ A row of hedges will be a good barrier against the wind and any outside disturbances.

NUTRITION

Berries are enjoyed by most birds. Feed only fresh food that you would eat yourself, not old or rotting items.

Proper nutrition is extremely important in maintaining the health and overall well being of your bird. Poor diet will result in a bird with limited energy and ambition and will make it more susceptible to disease and illness. The first important factor is providing a good seed mix. For budgerigars it will consist mainly of canary and millet seed, as well as niger, linseed, oats and hemp. Along with seed, a variety of fresh greens such as dandelion and spinach is also important, as well as some bits of fruit such as grapes or berries. Even if fresh fruits and greens are not readily accepted, keep offering them. Eventually, the bird will try different foods and begin to incorporate them into its diet. Unacceptance of these foods may happen when a bird has been fed strictly a seed diet.

In the wild, birds will eat half ripened seeds when available. They offer extra nutrition and are also easily digestible.

NUTRITION

A varied diet is the key to proper nutrition. Health cannot be achieved on one food item. ➧

Aviary and breeding birds require extra nutrition because they expend greater amounts of energy. In the wild, budgerigars rely on abundant green food around breeding time. This gives the birds more calcium, vitamins and minerals. Soaked bread with milk will give birds rearing young an easily digestible food to help them in the process.

▲ Greens are an important source of nutrition and are especially appreciated by breeding hens.

➧ There are many different types of treats available at your local pet shop that will add variety to your birds diet.

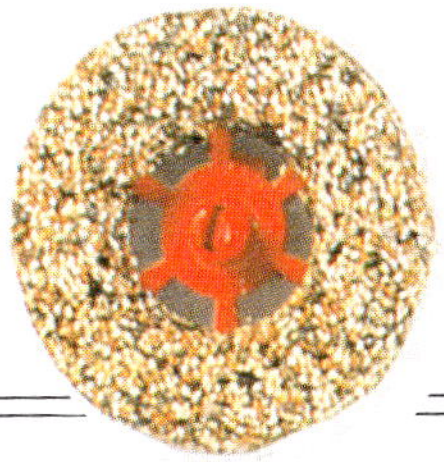

NUTRITION

Make sure seed dishes are always full. Do not just look at the dish to see, for it may be filled with just the hulls. Shake or blow the husks away and add fresh.

Soaked seed is especially advantageous to young, breeding or ailing birds, because of increased vitamin and protein levels. Take seeds of millet, wheat or oats and soak them overnight in water, then rinse well. Now they are ready for consumption! If the seeds smell musty or sour, DO NOT feed them to your birds.

If your bird does not accept fresh foods, vitamin and mineral supplements can be added to the seed or water. Check with your local pet supply store for their availability.

Be careful that your bird does not become obese. This condition is more likely in a household pet. If this happens, reduce fattening foods and offer more time outside of the cage for exercise.

Birds love spray millet which can be hung on the side of the cage or offered as soaked seed.

It may be harder to convince some birds that are used to an all seed diet to try new things, but offer it anyway.

Fresh clean water should be available at all times. Fresh twigs and branches are also important; best are ones of willow and fruit trees (except cherry). Cuttlebone and grit are also necessary additions that should not be overlooked.

If collecting foods and greens from the garden, make sure they have not been sprayed with insecticides. Wash all items thoroughly; gas exhaust can be harmful.

AS A PET

The most common pet bird today is the budgerigar. It is a hardy creature that is very adaptable and friendly. Don't forget to keep in mind the responsibility of owning a bird; if cared for properly it may live for well over ten years.

Before bringing your new bird home, you should have its cage set up in a proper location equipped with all the essentials. An area where the bird can be part of your daily living is ideal.

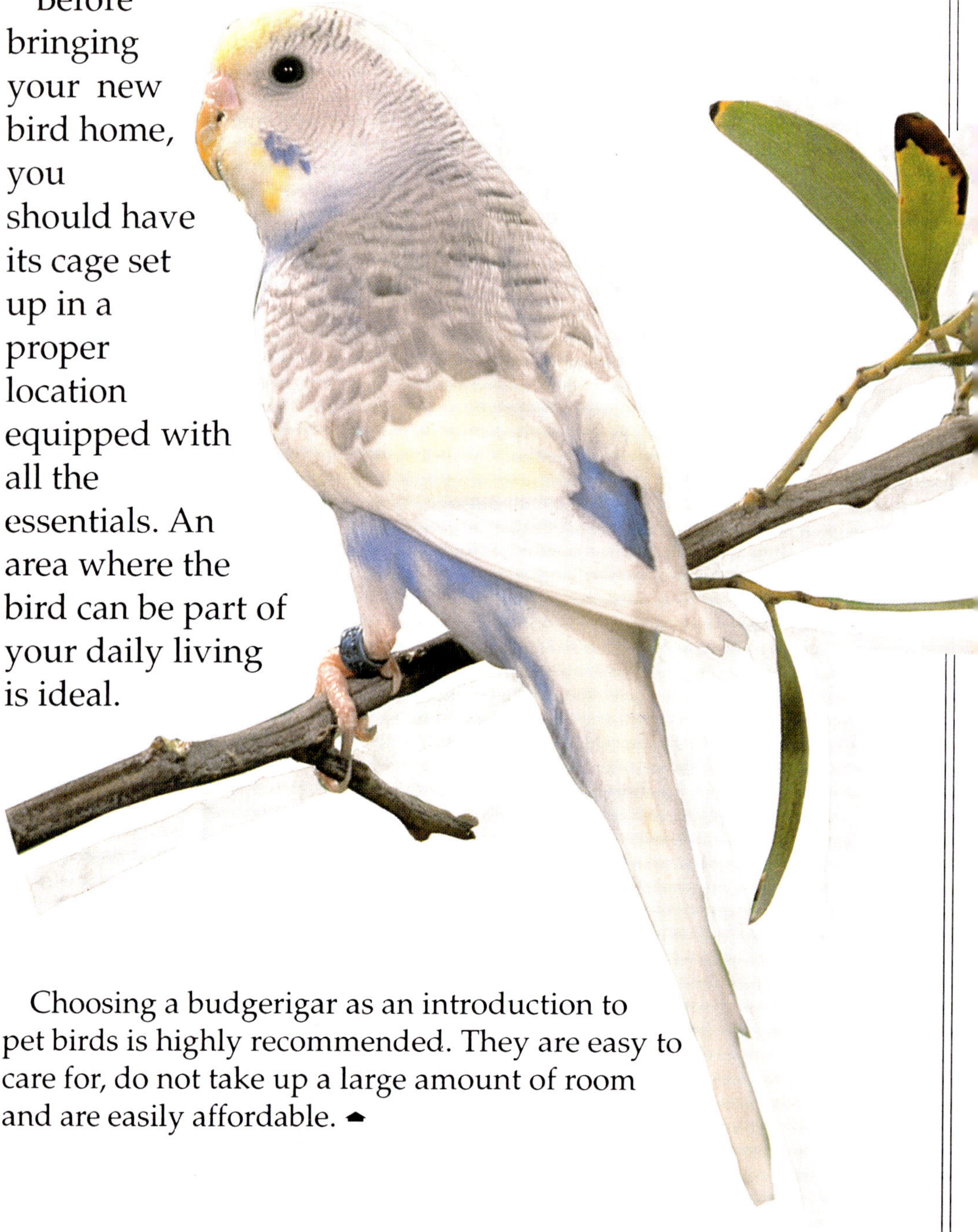

Choosing a budgerigar as an introduction to pet birds is highly recommended. They are easy to care for, do not take up a large amount of room and are easily affordable.

A suitable place for the cage is one that is free from drafts. Avoid placing the cage in front of a window, door or heating vent. Drafts and constant temperature changes can cause colds and respiratory illnesses. Never house a bird in the kitchen area. There will be temperature fluctuations as well as an abundant amount of odors. Also, if the bird should happen to be out of its cage while you are cooking it could be disastrous!

Do not place your bird in an area where it will sit in bright sunlight throughout the day. A place where it will receive natural light, but not direct sunlight, is best.

These are very social birds and if you feel that one will not get enough attention you may want to consider purchasing two birds.

AS A PET

Preening is the bird's way to keep its feathers clean and smooth.

Once you have found the perfect spot, position the cage so that it is at eye level. In the wild, danger comes from above and the birds will instinctively feel fearful if people are constantly hovering over them. After bringing the bird home, let it acclimate itself to its new environment for a week or two. After this time, if the bird is not acting nervous and is eating well, you can begin to take it out of the cage for exercise or taming sessions

You may wish to cover your bird's cage in the evening to provide it with undisturbed resting time, especially if you stay up late. This will assure that the bird gets enough rest to remain healthy and active.

AS A PET

Household plants may be poisonous to your bird. Make sure that all poisonous or questionable plants are removed when your bird is at liberty.

When letting your bird out of the cage for play and exercise, use caution. Exposed windows and mirrors should be covered; a bird may fly directly into them possibly causing itself great injury. Other household pets should not be present if you are unable to provide constant supervision. Make certain the bird is never left out and unattended. With these curious and playful creatures there is no telling what they will get into.

Budgies tame very easily and make wonderful companion birds.

Be sure to watch your bird carefully when it is unconfined; any item may pique its curiosity and become a plaything or something desirable to nibble on.

MAINTENANCE

Wing clipping is a procedure done by choice of a bird owner to limit or take away the ability of flight. The main reasons for clipping a bird's wings are for safety and ease of training. It can be done to keep a wild flier from injuring itself and will also be a precaution to a pet escaping out of an open door or window. It is very important in the taming process to keep the bird from flying away and aids in easy retrieval. A veterinarian or experienced aviculturist should perform this task for you or give you guidance until you feel comfortable with doing it yourself.

The outer couple of primaries can be left for appearance or all can be cut.

When clipping the wings, good light and sharp scissors are necessary. The feathers to be cut are the primary flight feathers, which are the outer ten feathers of the wing. Do not cut below the primary coverts.

From time to time claws may need to be trimmed. If the bird is supplied with natural branches as well as a cuttlebone they may never need to be clipped. When trimming nails, only the tip should be removed. There is a vein in the nail that can be seen in birds with light nail coloring. If you cut the nail too short you will hit the vein; if this happens press the nail into some styptic powder, which will help to stop the blood flow. If nails are grossly overgrown you will need to trim them more frequently until the desired length is achieved.

Natural branches will help keep nails trim by wearing them down. If allowed to become too long, nails may get hung up on one of the bird's toys or even the bars of the cage.

A pair of scissors or nail clippers can be used to cut the budgerigar's nails. Some birds will let their owners file the nails with a nail file, eliminating the chance of cutting a vein.

MAINTENANCE

Beaks may occasionally become overgrown and will need to be trimmed. This should be done very carefully with nail clippers or a nail file, depending on the amount that needs to be taken off. Overgrown beaks will make it difficult for the bird to properly groom its plumage and crack seeds. A veterinarian should be consulted first before attempting to do this on your own.

The beak should only be trimmed to aid the bird, never to just dull the bite.

If supplied with natural branches to gnaw on as well as a cuttlebone, the beak should remain in good condition throughout the life of the bird.

A nail file can be used to even and smooth out the beak after being trimmed.

BANDING

Banding birds is done as a means of identification. Bands are numbered and dated by year, therefore making it easy to determine when a bird was born. Other information can also be imprinted on bands if so desired.

There are two types of bands available, either closed or split rings. The latter are usually temporary and can be fitted onto either adults or chicks. Closed bands need to be fitted onto chicks when they are about five days old; shortly afterwards their toes become too large and the rings are unable to fit over them.

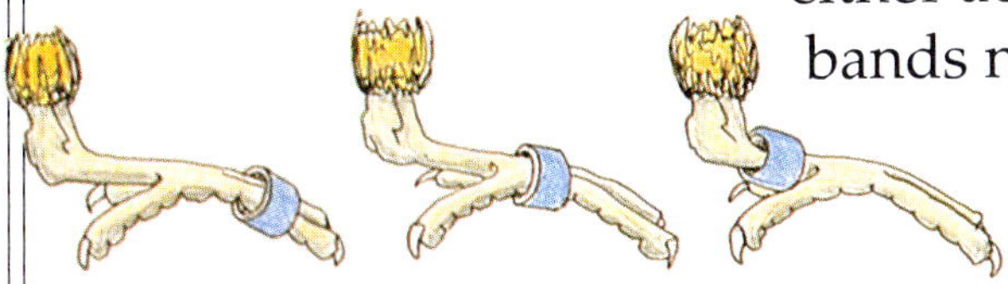

▲ To place a ring on a chick, slide the band over the front two toes and push up. The other two toes are then gently pulled through one at a time, starting with the smaller toe. A matchstick can aid in pulling the toes through the ring.

Bands are manufactured in different colors each year. This is helpful in determining the birth year of a bird in a cage or flight without having to catch it. ▶

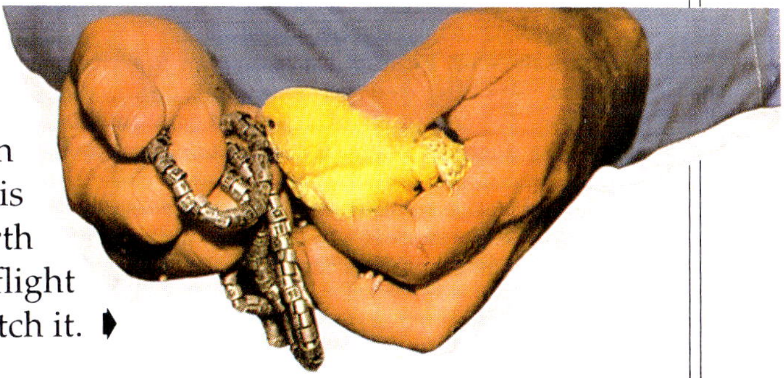

▼ After banding chicks, they should be checked frequently to make sure nothing has gotten caught between the band and the leg. If this happens, blood flow may be restricted and the bird can loose a foot. If the band needs to be removed for any reason, the aid of a veterinarian should be sought.

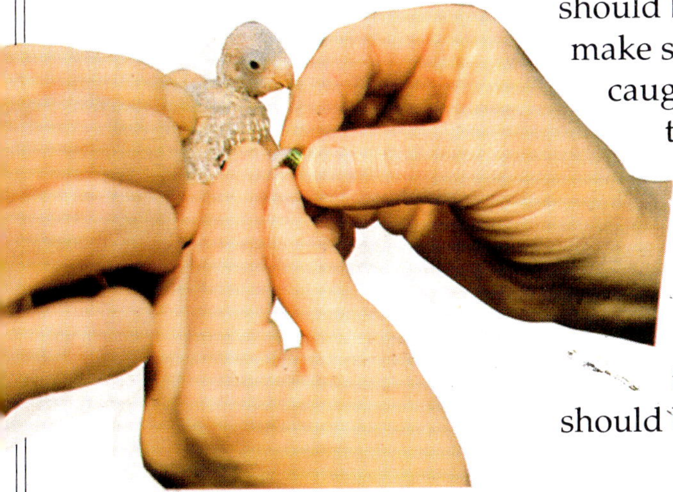

TAMING AND TRAINING

Before you begin the taming process it is a good idea to clip the bird's wings. This will reduce the amount of time spent chasing the bird and increase the time of the taming session. Choose a room that is small, uncluttered and free from distractions. Bring the cage in the room and open the door or take off the top so that the bird can come out on its own. To start, take a dowel or perch about twelve inches long and slowly bring it to the budgie, nudging lightly on its chest until it steps up onto the perch. It will probably try to avoid you at first, but if the wings are clipped it will soon tire of trying to run away. Repeat this until the bird seems comfortable with getting on and off the perch.

By lightly pushing on the chest, the bird will automatically step up onto the perch.

Budgies are one of the easiest birds to tame. Teaching it to perch on a dowel can easily be accomplished in just one session.

When teaching a bird to perch on your hand, keep it low to the ground so if it becomes frightened and jumps, it will not hurt itself.

Older budgies will require a little more patience and time, but they can still become playful family members.

TAMING AND TRAINING

To hand tame the bird, have it perch on the dowel and slowly bring your hand up nudging the chest so that it has to step up onto your hand. Since the budgie is usually an easy subject to tame, it will only take a session or two to hand tame a young bird. Once this is accomplished, you can easily gain its confidence and soon it will let you handle and pet it with no objections.

Daily training sessions will assure you a tame and trusting pet.

It is advantageous to have a tame bird, especially if it becomes injured or sick and needs to be handled.

Taming sessions should be conducted by the same person. Until the bird is fully comfortable and trusting of its trainer, other family members should not become involved.

TALKING

◖ Each lesson should be enjoyable for the bird. A favorite food as reward will give the bird positive reinforcement.

Budgerigars, like most other parrots, can learn to mimic sounds or talk. It is easiest when starting with a young bird, preferably a male; they seem to be superior to the females in this ability.

When starting to teach your bird to talk, begin with a very simple word such as 'hello' or possibly the bird's name if it is only one or two syllables. The voice of a woman or child is easier for the bird to imitate because of its higher pitch; keep this in mind when choosing who will be the bird's teacher.

◖ It may take a bird one week to learn to talk—or one year. Each individual has its own desire and ability to learn.

TALKING

Talking lessons should be held daily, preferably in the morning or early evening when the bird is most active. Make sure that there are no distractions present during the lesson, such as the TV, radio, other people or birds. All should be quiet so that you have the bird's full attention. The key to success is to repeat the word over and over. Do not try to mix words or try a new one before it has learned the first word completely. Only after it has mastered one word should you go on to another.

Some birds may learn a vocabulary of only three to four words, whereas others will learn much more, possibly including a few whistled tunes.

A tame bird will make a better learner because he already trusts you and considers you his companion.

Birds can learn sounds and say them on cue through association—for example, the ringing of a telephone and the word 'hello' immediately following.

HYGIENE

◆ When offering a bird bath, use water that is near room temperature, not hot or ice cold.

In the wild, budgerigars will bathe by rolling around on wet foliage until they are thoroughly wet or will take advantage of falling rains. Afterwards, birds will carefully preen their feathers. They will take into their beak fat from the oil gland and apply it to each feather. This helps to keep the feathers in good condition.

In caged birds, bathing from a bird bath is a learned habit and one to be enjoyed. They will also enjoy being sprayed lightly or even taking a shower under a slow running faucet. You may even offer wet grass or lettuce leaves for them to roll around in. Just remember to offer baths on sunny days, not damp chilly ones. It is best to offer baths in the morning or afternoon so that the bird can dry before evening, when the temperature will drop and the bird will be ready for bed.

◆ Aviary birds will often take advantage of a rain shower to clean their plumage.

◆ Bathing will help keep feathers clean, shiny and in top condition.

HYGIENE

The most important aspect of keeping a bird healthy is a clean environment. Cleaning and disinfecting the cage and perches weekly will keep it free from any bacteria and germs. The cage bottom is usually removable and should be cleaned more frequently. If using paper on the bottom of the tray, it can be replaced daily and will keep the cage looking neat. Wood shavings and corn cob bedding can also be used to line the bottom of the cage. These will soak up the moisture of the droppings and will not need to be changed daily.

A clean environment will keep your bird healthy and happy.

Even toys will become soiled and dirty and will need to be washed regularly.

If it becomes difficult to clean soiled perches, perch cleaners can be purchased at your local pet supply store. Sandpaper can be used to help scrape hardened droppings from natural branch perches.

A White cock budgerigar. Make sure that the cage and perches are completely dry before replacing the bird. Damp perches can chill the bird, making it ill.

HEALTH CARE

There may be certain times throughout the life of your bird when an accident may occur resulting in a wound or broken bone. It is best to be prepared ahead of time for any mishaps by having a first aid kit for your bird handy with the name and number of its veterinarian included. For minor cuts, washing the area and applying a non-toxic antiseptic or using a styptic powder to stop the bleeding will be all that is needed to treat the bird. For large or severe wounds, a call to the veterinarian is a must. In the event that the bird fractures a wing or leg, it should be placed in a warm hospital cage where it can be kept calm and quiet. The advice of a veterinarian should be sought. The bird may need to have a splint applied for proper healing.

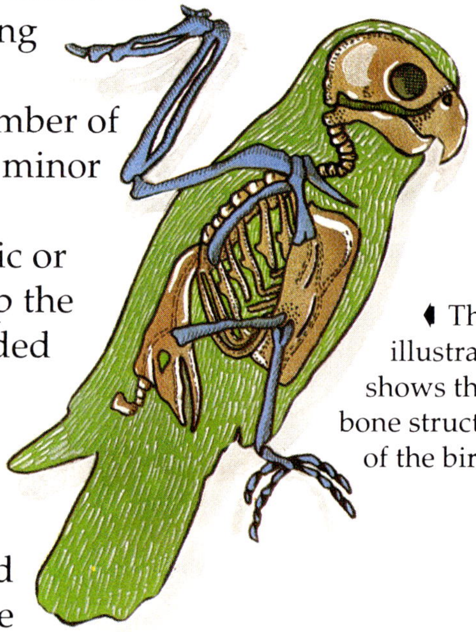

This illustration shows the bone structure of the bird.

Moulting is a yearly process in which the plumage is renewed. During this time you will not notice any gaps or bare patches in the plumage. It is a smooth transition in which new feathers will replace the old. During this time vitamin and mineral supplements should be provided because birds will have a lower resistance.

A travel cage is a must! It will let you transport your birds safely to the veterinarian in emergency and non-emergency situations.

Feather plucking is a problem in which there can be many causes. The most common reason for this is boredom. It is seen more in single pets which spend most of their time caged. Another cause can be a deficiency in the diet of the bird or even another bird may be the culprit. To try to alleviate the problem, offer more toys as well as natural branches so that it can gnaw and keep itself occupied. Spend more time with the bird and let it out for more exercise. Since diet can also be a factor, review what you are feeding it. Do you offer a variety of foods? You may want to offer a vitamin or mineral supplement as well. If you house birds together, remove the afflicted bird for it may be a cage mate who is responsible for the damage.

If unsure of your bird's health or condition, a trip to the vet may be a wise choice.

This bird shows an extreme result of feather plucking. All options to prevent this should have been taken, and even then, some will persist with no cause or cure being determined.

These newly emerging feathers are covered in a chalky white protective sheath.

CONDITIONING

Start to condition budgerigars at least two months before breeding. If proper conditioning is not allowed, it may result in problems for the hen. The hen may fail to produce fertile eggs, become eggbound or the chicks may be sickly.

◆ Birds in breeding condition will have smooth ceres and be in healthy, full plumage.

◆ It is best not to offer nest boxes until the birds are in breeding condition.

Pairs should get plenty of time to adjust in their new environment as well as a steady increase of protein in their diet. Soaked seed and green food should also be readily available. It will be of great value in rearing healthy chicks.

CONDITIONING

The cere of the hen will turn brown during breeding season.

A varied diet with increased amounts of high protein foods will maintain the bird's top condition during the breeding and chick rearing processes. The birds will use up more energy during this time.

The addition of a mineral supplement is beneficial, as is cuttlebone, calcium blocks, oyster shells and grit. The production of strong egg shells and bones depend on the amounts of calcium the female bird receives.

These young budgies should not be bred until they are at least twelve months old; although they will reach sexual maturity at about four months of age.

Preening each other is part of courtship behavior, which is usually initiated by the cock.

SEXING AND PAIRING

Sexual maturity is reached rather early in budgerigars. Although they mature by about 4 to 5 months of age, wait until they are at least a year or little older before breeding, so as not to put too much strain on the hen. This will assure a longer breeding life of the female. In the wild they breed in colonies and need stimulation from other members of the flock, so it is best to start with at least two pairs. If starting with younger birds, you may have a difficult time sexing certain individuals, so try to purchase 2 or 3 hens and 4 to 6 males and let them pair off themselves. If any mistakes are made in sexing, you still have a good chance of at least one or two couples.

It is best to let birds pair themselves in order to have completely compatible couples.

When pairing, a female will usually choose an older male as a mate.

SEXING AND PAIRING

When sexing mature birds, the first characteristic to look at would be the cere. If it is blue, it will be a male. If it is a chalky white color, brown, pinkish or even pale blue, it will be a female. Females also show thin white rings around each nostril.

When birds are permitted to select their own mate, fertility is usually improved. ➧

⬅ If breeding for certain color varieties, knowing the genetic background of your pairs is essential.

In young birds, before their first molt, the cere of the female will be a pale blue color and pinkish in young males. In certain color varieties, like lutinos, albinos, recessive pieds and red-eyed fallows, it will remain pinkish in the males. In the females of these varieties, the cere will be a pale blue except during breeding season when it will turn brown.

When trying to set up breeding pairs, place any unproven stock with partners that have previously reared chicks. Try not to pair unproven birds together. ➧

NESTING

Budgies can be bred in colonies or in pairs, inside cages or aviaries. Aviaries provide a more natural environment and are beneficial for the birds. They need the stimulation of other budgies for best results. In the wild, they are cavity nesters, as are all parrot species with the exception of one. Nesting material is not used, except for some accumulation of wood chips and debris that line the bottom of the shallow depression scraped by the bird at the bottom of the cavity. In captivity, nest boxes are used. Budgie nest boxes should have a small indented cavity already present; this will keep the eggs situated together.

In the wild, budgerigars nest in tree hollows.

A nest box with a hinged roof will allow one to inspect the nest with minimal disturbance to the hen or chicks.

If a nest box has been previously used, it should be completely disinfected before being offered to another pair.

NESTING

Suitable nest boxes can be purchased from a local retailer or built. A suitable size is one of about 9x9x6 inches. A hinged top will make it easier to inspect the nest if needed. The opening of the box should be just big enough for the bird to get in and out, and can be placed in the middle or to one side. An opening off to the side will allow the hen to lay the eggs out of a draft and may make her feel more secure. A perch should be placed just below the opening on the outside to allow the pairs to easily enter the box. A perch or ladder can be provided inside the box to make it easier for the female to exit the nest, and also the chicks when they are able.

▲ A perch below the opening of the nest box will allow the pair to check on their young, and will also make it easier for the male to feed the female during the incubation period.

▼ After mating, the female will start to spend more time inside the nest box.

▲ Place at least two nest boxes per pair in aviaries to give your birds a choice. This couple consists of an Opaline Cobalt Budgerigar and a Pied Cobalt Budgerigar.

EGG LAYING

Egglaying will begin about fourteen days after the mating process. The average clutch is from 4 to 6 eggs, with one being laid every other day. The hen will not begin incubating until the second egg is laid. The hen is responsible for incubating the eggs; although the male will occasionally join her. During this time, the male will feed the female so that she will not have to leave the nest.

After about eighteen days hatching will begin. Birds will hatch with the aid of a sharp egg tooth, which protrudes from the end of the beak. This is lost shortly after hatching. Sometimes, a day or so before hatching, chirping can be heard from inside the unhatched egg.

This is an average budgerigar clutch, but they can lay as few as two eggs or as many as nine.

Eggs will hatch approximately every other day in the same sequence in which they were laid.

These three day old chicks will grow rapidly, being ready to leave the nest in about four weeks.

EGG LAYING

For the first few days of life, the hen is solely responsible for feeding the chicks. The hen will feed her chicks a secretion called crop-milk. This is a protein rich food regurgitated from the proventriculus or stomach, not from the crop as the name would imply.

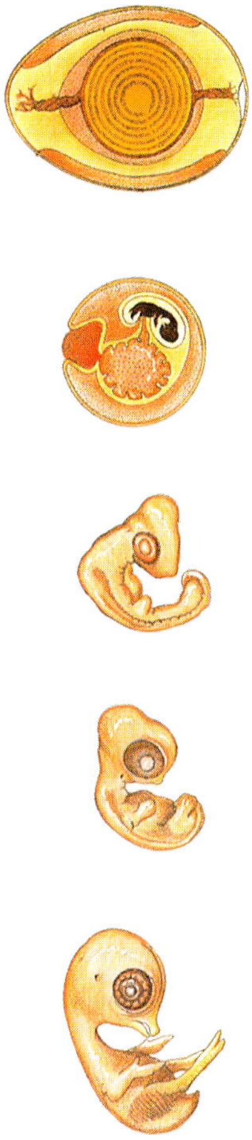

These illustrations show the stages of development of a budgerigar chick inside the egg.

Proper humidity is very important to the unhatched eggs. If it is too low, the eggs will become dry and the chicks will be unable to hatch out.

A hen with three of her hatchlings. Notice the difference in size between the three youngsters.

CHICK REARING

For the first few days after hatching, only the female feeds the nestlings from predigested food from the stomach, after which the male will join in. Normal colored chicks will develop mouse grey down, where the lighter colored strains will have white down. They depart from the nest at approximately 4 to 5 weeks of age, at which time they are fully feathered. Once out in the aviary, they very rarely return to the nest. The male will continue to feed the fledged young for another 1 to 2 weeks.

During this time he would have shown his chicks the feed dishes and how to eat seed for themselves. After they leave the nest, the female no longer shows any interest in the young and she is usually already starting a new clutch.

Newly hatched chicks of any parrot species, like this cockatoo, will begin chirping to let the female know that it's time to eat.

Fluffy down will cover the chicks' body after about eight days.

CHICK REARING

The pairs should not be allowed to raise more than three clutches per year. Overbreeding will create an unnecessary strain on the birds, leaving them exhausted and leading to poor health. Their clutches will be smaller as will the chicks. This will shorten the years of a good breeding pair. Proper and thoughtful management are necessary in keeping your birds healthy and in top condition, so that they may continue being productive.

◖ Both parents will care for the youngsters until they leave the nest, at which time the male will continue to feed the chicks for another couple weeks.

◖ Here you will be able to notice which birds hatched first. They grow rapidly; a day or two can make a sizeable difference in development.

BREEDING PROBLEMS

Breeders of budgerigars will come across certain problems at one time or another. Through knowledge and practicing good maintenance and care skills, you will have fewer problems.

The failure of eggs hatching is one problem that can have many different causes. The most common cause is infertile eggs. This can be the result of birds not being in breeding condition, incompatible pairs, environmental conditions being poor or even a genetic problem. Other reasons eggs may not hatch can be that the embryo , through some defect, does not fully develop or the shell is too thick for the chick to hatch from. This may mean that the hen was not properly nourished. Also, the humidity may have been too low or too high.

BREEDING PROBLEMS

Eggbinding is another problem in which the hen cannot pass an egg. A hen will look distressed, usually sitting on the floor of the cage all fluffed up. This will require immediate attention because eggbinding can be fatal. If this is observed, remove the hen and put her in a heated cage. Sometimes a warmer environment will help the egg pass. If this does not help, a few drops of oil gently massaged into the vent may help. If the egg is not passed in about an hour, consult your vet immediately. If a hen has a problem like this, wait at least a year before breeding again.

The need for proper nutrition can not be stressed strongly enough, especially during breeding season when more proteins, vitamins and minerals are needed.

These beautiful birds are the examples of well cared for stock.

Some hens may sustain internal damage with eggbinding and should not be bred. Instead, they should lead the life of a pet.

Many situations can be avoided through proper nutrition, environmental conditions and by knowing your birds. The more knowledge you attain will help you to avoid any unnecessary setbacks in your breeding program.

SHOW AND EXHIBITION

Exhibiting your birds at local shows may be another way to become involved in the budgerigar hobby. Show standards can be acquired through your local bird club, as well as a listing of shows scheduled for your area. It is not as easy as picking up your bird and carting it off to a scheduled show; you must carefully select a specimen as close to the given standards as possible. Many breeders are also exhibitors, so you may want to consult with some of them before making any purchases. Attend a few shows first to find out what is entailed in exhibiting budgies.

There is a standard that is strived for in exhibition birds. A point system is used to judge many characteristics, such as its condition, size, throat spots, head and tail, to name a few.

Training at an early age is important so that they become accustomed to the show cage, which are all alike, as well as to other people and birds without shying away.

Sometimes a bird may need to be cleaned before a show if the feathers have become soiled. These birds must be in top condition with perfect feathers and no defects, such as missing toes.

SHOW AND EXHIBITION

Before exhibiting a bird it must become accustomed to the show cage so that it feels totally at home. It must also be trained not to shy away or cower in a corner when strangers approach. ◗

Show cages are painted black on the outside, white on the inside and must be in immaculate condition. The floor should be covered with seed. The bird also has to be in top condition with perfect, clean feathering, as well as an overall appearance of superior health. You may decide that showing is not for you, but that doesn't mean that you can't enjoy the companionship of these truly captivating and endearing birds.

◖After returning from a show, the bird should be isolated from others to make sure that it has not caught any illness from any other stock that were exhibited. The cage should be cleaned and disinfected so that it is ready for the next time you wish to use it.

Not all birds show the traits that will make it a successful show specimen. These may be excellent breeders and will certainly make great pets. ◗

DISEASE AND ILLNESS

The first step in helping your bird recover from any illness is to learn to tell when your bird is not feeling well. Birds that are sick will show a decrease in activity and sometimes a loss of appetite. They will usually sit all fluffed up with eyes closed. The head will hang and both feet will be gripping the perch.

The most common cause of illness in a bird are drafts, which can cause a cold and respiratory problems. Antibiotics that can be administered into the drinking water are available to treat minor colds.

There can also be many other illnesses in which a bird will exhibit the same symptoms. Because many sicknesses have similar symptoms, a veterinarian should be consulted right away. Fecal and blood samples are sometimes necessary to help a veterinarian in determining a diagnosis.

Internal parasites such as tapeworms are more likely to occur in aviary birds. Samples of droppings should be checked by a veterinarian yearly to insure that your birds stay free from infestation.

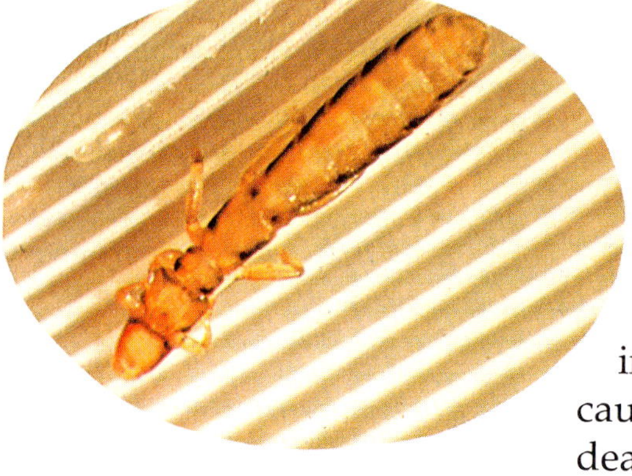

A close-up of a mite on the feather of a bird. Severe infestation of these parasites is cause for major concern, and can be deadly in extreme cases.

DISEASE AND ILLNESS

Always be aware of your bird's condition, this will help you notice when your bird is not well. The earlier you detect that something is wrong the better, for the condition of an ill bird can deteriorate quickly. ➧

Parasites are another cause of sickness in birds. External parasites such as lice and mites will live in the nooks and crannies of the cage and perches. These parasites are blood suckers and can cause the birds to become anemic. They can be avoided through proper and frequent cleaning of the cage and surrounding environment. If infestation occurs, treatment is available at pet supply stores in the manner of sprays and powders.

Scaly face and scaly leg are caused by mites too, but just in different parts of the body. These parasites bury themselves deep in the skin. The affected areas will become encrusted and flaky. It can be treated effectively when detected early.

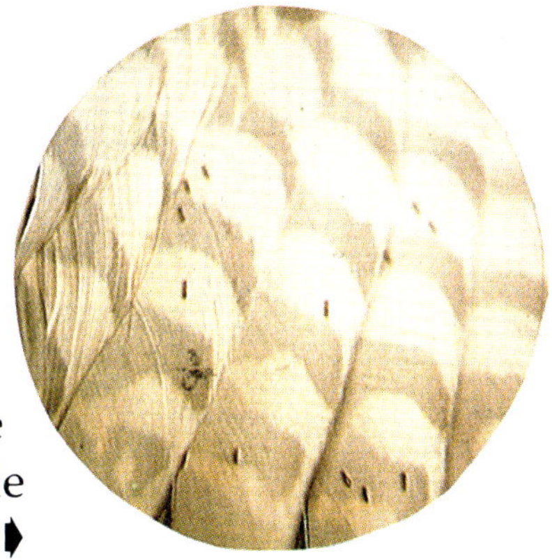

This picture shows the presence of feather mites on the underside of a birds' wing. ➧

DISEASE AND ILLNESS

If left to progress in the face, the beak will become brittle with holes appearing. Unfortunately, at this advanced stage, the bird may starve because it will be unable to eat with such a defective beak.

French moult is a disease that appears in young budgerigars which causes abnormal feather growth. Stunted feather growth and excessive moulting makes it impossible for these birds to fly well, if at all, so are termed 'runners'. The general health of these birds are otherwise unaffected except in severe cases. A devastating disease for all parrots is psittacosis. Many times there are no clinical signs of the disease in the carriers or infected birds. When symptoms do appear, they usually start out as colds, causing diarrhea, runny eyes and nostrils, as well as coughing.

This bird is suffering from French Moult. Notice the stunted feather growth of the wings and the bald patch on the back. Before reaching full size, many quills will fall out.

The abnormal shape of the beak in this bird is caused by the scaly face mite.

DISEASE AND ILLNESS

This is the proper way to restrain your bird if you need to examine it closely.

This specimen is in sound physical condition.

Other signs are those of listlessness, loss of appetite, weight loss, quick, labored and wheezy breathing which can result in the death of the bird. Since this is a highly contagious disease that can even affect humans, it should be reported immediately to your veterinarian should you suspect an outbreak.

A cage in which a bird can be isolated from others in case of any illness will prove to be handy. It will also make transportation easier if a visit to the vet is required.

Notice the encrusted skin on the cere and flaky upper mandible of this budgerigar suffering from scaly face.

INDEX

Page numbers in **boldface** refer to illustrations.